Another Morning

poems by

William Minor

Finishing Line Press
Georgetown, Kentucky

Another Morning

*For Betty, Tim, Shannon, Steve, Yoko, Emily, Blake,
Megan & Michelle—of Course*

Copyright © 2020 by William Minor
ISBN 978-1-64662-115-6 First Edition
All rights reserved under International and Pan-American Copyright Conventions. No part of this book may be reproduced in any manner whatsoever without written permission from the publisher, except in the case of brief quotations embodied in critical articles and reviews.

ACKNOWLEDGMENTS

Homestead Review: "Another Morning," "The Delights of Age," "Time," "On Reading, after Long Absence, the Poems of Charles Peguy," and "Falling in Love," Fall issue, 2018
Monterey Poetry Review: "Full of It," "Another Love Song," May 2017
Red Wheelbarrow: "Names," Volume 17, 2016
YouTube: "Another Morning by William Minor," https://www.youtube.com/watch?v=epJ7eFylCoQ

Publisher: Leah Maines
Editor: Christen Kincaid
Cover Art and Design: William Minor
Author Photo: Stephen Minor
Cover Design: Elizabeth Maines McCleavy

Printed in the USA on acid-free paper.
Order online: www.finishinglinepress.com
        also available on amazon.com

Author inquiries and mail orders:
Finishing Line Press
P. O. Box 1626
Georgetown, Kentucky 40324
U. S. A.

Table of Contents

Names 1

Genesis 2

The Delights of Age 3

Another Morning 6

Our Dance 7

Time 8

On Reading, after Long Absence, the Poems of Charles Peguy ... 10

Falling in Love 12

Just the Way It Is 13

Full of It 16

Another Love Song 18

Homo Poeta 19

Just Sit There 21

Poetry 23

The Sounds of Kauai 25

NAMES

Having just watched *Tarzan the Ape Man*
(1932) and *Tarzan and His Mate* (1934),
my wife of sixty years and I have begun
to communicate in a unique new way:
"Me," I say, tapping her lightly on the chest,
and, "No," she says, "*I'm* me." "Me," I say,
tapping her on the chest again, because
it feels so good that way; and she says, "No,"
again: "I'm me, you you." "*You?*" I say,
tapping my own chest, and she says, "No,
you are *you* and I am *me*," and just when
it seems we are finally getting somewhere
after sixty years together, I say, "Me Tarzan,
you Jane," and she laughs and says, tapping
my chest not quite so lightly, "Not Tarzan ...
Bill!" And totally confused now, I say,
"You Bill?" And she says, "*You* Bill, me
Betty," and I say, "Love?" And smiling,
she says, "Yes, love." I say, "*Me?*" And she
says, "Yes, you." "Me too," I say, "you."
And finally we agree on something.

Tarzan/Bill, it's all the same, just as
it is with Betty/Jane; for sixty years
of swinging on vines and trees
in our very own forest has taught us
there is so much more to love than you
can find in fancy words, or any name.

GENESIS

All our lives begin and end
with music; the sea itself
was silent, sleeping, and then
awoke in song.

Or maybe the goddess
Aphrodite, arising from foam
sang us into birth so she might
find release from her own longing.

However we began (perhaps
as simple chemistry,
a primal soup that came
aground to sing of love?),

we began and we shall end
as music—for our story
can only be told with faith
that finds its voice in song.

THE DELIGHTS OF AGE

Just one portion of my body seems
to be working as it should now:
the *newest* part, the only portion
that's solely *current*: the right knee
the bone marrow of which has been
created from scratch by way of a process
called Subchondroplasti, but ...
this beautiful (functional) new knee
is the only part of my eighty-three
year old body that doesn't complain
on a daily (and nightly) basis of pain
or displeasure of one sort or another.

My left foot suffers from neuropathy
(nerve damage); both calves are swollen
with edema (water retention) and I
now set high standards for fashion
by wearing brightly-colored corrective
stockings day and night.

                         Moving
upward (on this tour of the temple, my body),
I still have two knees, both of which
have accumulated their share
of surgeries (meniscus tears three
times, and the process I mentioned)—
and my groin? Well, forget it! "I'm over
the hump," as a comedian once quipped.
My stomach makes noises (groans and
growls) that resemble a truck with a failed
catalytic converter; I have an umbilical hernia,
and GERD (gastroesophageal reflux
disease) to boot, which requires
me to clear phlegm from my throat
and qualifies me as the perfect
adjunct to any party; and my belly

has mastered a pretty good imitation
of a whale when it comes to appetite
and size.

       My lungs are relatively
intact (some mild wheezing, and
a propensity to become bronchitic
at the drop of a hat; I've had pneumonia
three times in my life). I'm all heart
when it comes to feelings, and the pump
itself works on occasion (although I've
had to work hard to keep my blood
pressure down where it belongs). Right shoulder?
Bursitis. Vestibular system? Tinnitus
and permanent damage to my inner ear
(vertigo, for twenty-seven years now).
Oh yes, and to top it all off: constant sinusitis.

Eyesight compromised (age-related
macular degeneration and ocular migraine;
but compensation: should things get worse,
I just may play piano as well as Ray Charles).
My vocal chords are in good shape, for I
can still SING! SING! SING! An activity
I relish, and live for: any kind of song,
from jazz to blues to folk to opera to show
tunes. And thank God, I can still
TALK. TALK, TALK, TALK!
(about almost *anything*; you name it!)

But I refuse to take requests when
I sing (and play piano); well, I might do
"Aint' Misbehavin,'" "The Nearness
Of You," or "As Time Goes By."

I forgot to mention my hands, which,
although arthritic, are mostly OK

(when I play! And thank God for *that*
again!). One of my favorite songs is
The Avett Brothers' "No Hard Feelings"
(perfection: words and music, along with
Seth's voice, and soul). I have no
enemies but myself—and I'm learning how
to live with him (myself), with resigned
affability. I have no hard feelings
for what my body (my temple) has
been put through or put me through; no Sir.
No hard feelings at all. Just gratitude
for the gift of life with all it makes us bear
for the sake of knowing we are worthy of it.

                      And we are.
And we are. And we are: a three-tag tune
with which to end this poem—with thanks
(the only prayer that should suffice)
for my one healthy preserve: my brand
new knee—and maybe the rest of me too.

ANOTHER MORNING

What once came with ease
has been placed on hold,
but I still like to get up
in the morning
to a woman and a world
I'm lucky to discover
on another day of sunlight or rain.

I take to my feet, and
the effort feels good
albeit cautious, and slow—
yet the trek to the kitchen
is all it takes to make
me grateful to find
the woman whose heart I still love.

We no longer need to count
the years we have been
together, because duration
that makes up this moment belongs
to us alone, as one another.

So we sit together now
and you read a book
and I think whatever thoughts
I can—nothing resolved but
your presence here with me
in this sacred room: a simple
kitchen where we live
to love for one more day.

OUR DANCE

Once upon a time we danced
to a crowd's applause, homegrown
of course, colleagues of yours—
many of whom claimed they came
to the annual party just to watch
us dance the way we did.

Not clones of Ginger and Fred,
we were just ourselves, ordinary
folk who loved the feel of bodies,
our own, agile in flight within
a world of splayed light that
played upon a parquet floor.

The tunes didn't matter, the tempo
did: not too fast, and when slow
melodiously so; we faced whatever
music, and let it dwell in us
within the depth of another night.

Now, we stay at home and dance
in comfortable chairs, alone but
not lonely, for once known, the dance
that was ours can never end, but lives
within two souls, aging cheek to cheek,
and with feet that can still sing.

TIME

Why do we need it so? It doesn't even exist,
unless we make it happen by consulting
a watch, or wait for the sun to go down—
which is just what I am doing now, but trying
not to count time, whatever portion of it
I've been out here in the back yard. The sun
feels *just right* on my face: a warm bath
of bliss, the caress of heat—so splendid,
so consoling, so benign, I did not think
to count at all until just now, when
the wind came up and I began to feel
the chill, and realized the sun *was* going
down (or doing whatever it does
to remove itself, eventually, from view).

But what *time* is it? Sunset?
Twilight? Nightfall? Dusk? Just the *death*
of another day? That's all too dramatic,
because I bet I have at least another
hour, or two, or even eternity before I
call this a day (Friday the 13th,
by the way, and it's April, "the cruelest
month")—so *stay*, sun! Stay! I command
(as Mayakovsky might, or would);
but the sun pays no attention to me at all,
nor has it any reason to.

I sit here
for a few more ... minutes? Hours?
Centuries? Eternities? And *nothing*
seems to pass (not even time!), nor grow
colder now; I just sit beside a garden,
beneath a sky, the sound of airplanes
singing overhead, just sit in ...time?
Whatever it is, I *never* want to leave
this state, so at home in it am I.

                              I could
call it God's time, eternity, if it's
time at all, but that sounds pretentious,
so I settle for this prolonged *sit*, feeling
warm within the emerging cold
and the descent of the sun, but in no
hurry, feeling no haste at this demise,
the sun's or my own, or the death
of anything. I just *sit* here, perfectly
still, perfectly content, and sip a glass
of wine, and then another (Why count
how many—an act that takes *time*?). I begin
to wonder why my wife is taking so long
shopping, but that concern too is irrelevant.

The evening sun goes down behind
the telephone wires and darkening trees
I love, and only the chill of evening
will take me back inside the house,
but not the passage of time.

ON READING, AFTER LONG ABSENCE, THE POEMS OF CHARLES PEGUY

Who would dare, innocently, to adopt,
as an alter ego, the voice of God? Charles Peguy,
who was born where Bishop Saint Aignan
curtailed the progress of Attila the Hun
in the Fifth century, and where Joan of Arc
would, a thousand years later, make her stand.
Charles Peguy, a poet whose father died
when he was still a baby, and whose mother
made a living for the family mending chairs—
a task Peguy himself was very good at:
this poet who called himself a "peasant" long after
he failed to graduate (having tried several times)
from the Ecole Normale in France, and who
was, at the age of forty-one, shot in the forehead
leading his troops (in a conspicuous red and blue
uniform) through the hell of Villery, shells
bursting all around them. He died there.

Charles Peguy, who left behind a world
of poetry I would discover when I was
nineteen years of age, and was moved to faith
by the opening lines of "The Passion of Our Lady,"
in which the parents of Christ confess, "It was
their fault," for they "had always been too proud
of him." They ruthlessly explained that, throughout
his "brilliant" display of learning before the doctors,
he should have been more careful, because "people
like that have good memories" (otherwise they
would never have become doctors), and he
"must have hurt their feelings that day."

Charles Peguy. Where and how, in your peasant
soul, did you find the insight to write, as God speaks,
"When you love someone, you love him as he is;"
or as a God who recognizes perfection (because
He is perfect himself), knowing how difficult
it is to attain—requires less of it from others:
aware they will never learn to swim should He
always hold them above water—a God who sees
not only the deepest ocean and darkest forest,
but "the deep heart of man" as well; a God
who has witnessed "beading tears" of love that shall
outlast "the stars in heaven"; a God who knows
"whole lives from birth to death," unwinding like
a "skein of wool," yet finds nothing so beautiful
as a child falling asleep saying prayers, and laughing
happily, not even knowing what those prayers
are all about.

          Charles Peguy. Like him I only
pray while walking the streets or riding a bus,
not in a church—for if God is not *everywhere*,
and speaks not *here* as well as in heaven,
He is nowhere at all. And that would be
a crying shame, in the eyes of Charles Peguy
and in these eyes of mine which still can see
"nights that follow each other and are linked,"
continuous, like the "innermost part" of our
being, the being in which we bathe, are nourished,
were created, in which all we are was made.

Source: *God Speaks*
Charles Peguy
Translation by Julian Green

FALLING IN LOVE

> *"Loved ones will break your heart*
> *With or without you."*
> The Avett Brothers, *"Smithsonian"*

Another extra-large human irony:
the all-consuming state of having
fallen in love takes over, everything—
and eventually will even exclude
the object of love, the loved one,
from its domain.

      Perhaps we are
much more than we know we are—
truly capable of loving someone
for their actuality, and staying
on course for a lifetime—but we
seem to settle for less, feeling
there's only room enough in love
for the act of loving itself.

      Something, or someone
has *got to go*, and that's the beloved, because
the subject, ourselves, is in love with love—
no person but a condition, like a head cold
bed rest alone might cure: solitude, drawn
curtains in an attic chamber we inhabit
alone, dreaming of perfect love—
with or without an object, a loved one,
to distract us from the commitment.

JUST THE WAY IT IS

> *"All that is made perfect by progress perishes also by progress."*
> Pascal

1.

"It's just the way it is," I say
to myself, and that's something
I try to believe at my
advanced age: an article
of faith, a state of being—
and then I realize the phrase
matches the meter exactly
of "You must remember this,
a kiss is just a kiss"—a line
from one of my favorite
songs: "As Time Goes By."

Such sudden insight makes
the phrase, the state of being
I've embraced at this senescent
age appear as ambivalent as
it is, for nothing is "just
the way it is"; everything is
as much or as little as we
make it, and anything inside
can find its way outside
into possibility; or what's
outside take up Trappist-seclusion
residence within.

Outside/inside has replaced
body/soul as the fundamental
"truth" of things, and their
marriage, their ultimate union
is the condition to which
we now aspire: a quantum
shower of particles (or waves)
which we, as observers (and actors)

determine the outcome of.

"And which suit will I wear tonight?
Take out the brown, but in the end
wear the white?" Either way,
I shall step out into the light.

2.

One must retain everything,
and move on with "a horror of life
and a love of it," in the words
of Russian poet Alexander Blok,
who felt both disgust at human beings
and attraction to them, "the vanity
of art and its necessity."

Blok settled for reality, clarity,
ecstasy, acceptance, sadness—
the full spectrum, from dismal
to glad—sometimes simultaneously,
for "joy and suffering are one."

I long to live thus, passionately,
the *full course* of existence,
and not a reconstructed replica.
I long to live with simple, heady,
pleasant possibilities: to converse
with fellow beings at "an increasingly
deep level," make a genuine
connection with the universe—
and rub shoulders with *all*
that can be said to exist.

3.

I would embrace the daily grind
as if it were music and answer
for myself alone, yet also respond
in words that return as a song
sung by many voices, from
many mansions, hovels, huts,
tents, and humble homes: "I am
with you, you will not walk alone"—
for we each carry immortal flux,
criss-crossing connections that
just won't settle for temporal reward,
but reside within ambient harmony
that contains all the sounds
that surround us; the music of
a future we cannot capture
on a thumb drive—being *this*,
just the way it is as time goes by.

FULL OF IT

The empty space that is my mind—
so teased and tempted by all
those bittersweet love songs
that have made up my life, minute by minute,
hour by hour, night after night:
an intrusion on reflection,
on meditative moments that should
consist of nothing but the absence
of anything to mediate upon—
these have been matched by
the incursion of beautiful, blond,
bare-shouldered strangers with
dubious call-girl charm, such as
Allye who, when asked about the work
she does, replies, "I move around a lot."

Allye, in whom (I suspect) the presence
of anything resembling timeless
meditation does not loom large,
but whose accidental company I do
enjoy until she hastens off to catch
the Westbound Departure Train
to New York City, leaving Old Saybrook,
Connecticut, a place in which (I did
discover) she was born: a place
in which I do not live, am just
visiting—sipping espresso
at Ashlawn Farms Coffee.

    A minute or so
later, Allye returns, and smiles, and states,
"I forgot my phone," which she retrieves
inside. "Can't live without it," I say
when she comes out, employing my
best user friendly voice (I do not own
a smart phone), returning her smile.
We say "Goodbye" again, and I watch
her slender perfect backside presence
wander off to the train station, again.

      All this time,
love songs have been playing over
a speaker, softly, at Ashlawn Farms:
"Moonlight in Vermont," "Georgia,"
"I've Got a Crush on You," "Misty,"
"Guess Who I Saw Today," "You Don't Know
What Love Is" ("You don't know how
hearts burn / For love that cannot live,
yet never dies."), "Don't Go to Strangers,"
and "Until The Real Thing Comes Along."

      Slowly, I
sip the rich kiss of espresso and attempt
to return to a meditative state—retreat
to those empty spaces of my mind,
leaving just enough intentionality alive
to record the words of this poem.

ANOTHER LOVE SONG

We search for Lara throughout our lives
and ultimately find she has existed
all along, right before our eyes; embodied
in the woman long by our side.

The search for Lara was a temporal state,
a tease, only what fate intended to provide
some other me, compelled to search forever
for a Lara beyond his means.

I cannot credit you with having had a hand
in this, my Love, for you have always been
who you are, oblivious to the joy of being *you*
and the joy you inspire in others.

So Dear One, please stay in that humble state,
in which you embody all the Laras that may
or may not exist for someone I may have
wished to be, but never was.

HOMO POETA

After, and in homage to, Ernest Becker

Too many times recently, I have ignored
or abstained from the daily celebration
I should take comfort in: the many
wondrous petty occasions that make it all
worthwhile, livable—and I
apologize for this sin of omission,
the forgetfulness we are err to,
the reservoir of meaning evaporating
before our very eyes.

Too little
"shared performances"—and it's
my own damn fault, this paucity
of mutual dream; the ideal substance
sapped, so many hollow hours left
in between—no synoptic view, or
"vue d'ensemble."

I stay indoors,
I shun others: that world of agonism,
"strutting appearances," envy, acquisition,
a divisive world, disruptive, composed
of greed and self-display, a world
in which "appear" has replaced "to be."

Thankfully, I do have the privacy
a loved object affords; I do have *you*:
a tangible means of imparting meaning
we all seek, the instinct to create
something larger than ourselves—
"more valid than the best we can put forth."

Transformation! Transcendence!
The only games in town worth playing,
those and multiplicity of purpose,
ourselves "subordinated to existence itself"—
but please excuse this host of abstractions,
even though they strike me as being
as close to "true" as we can ever get.

              I long to be playful
as the Middle Ages (though not as cruel),
fat with the flavor, the style, the dignity
of ritual dance, a knight forever on
his silver horse, but never off to war,
existing only to serve his Lady,
just as I (my well-centered yet still
mysterious wife) serve you. Together
we shall take possession of the world,
and stage *our own* mutual drama "as only
it can be staged"—

              banners unfurled;
"more inner spirit in the hard world of things,"
loyalty and devotion restored in hearts
alive with perpetual music, ours,
ours, and ours alone—living with sublime
intensity in our own "expansive present,"
a larger promise in concert not contention;
living fully the daily round—another
comfortable morning, afternoon, or evening
in a genuine kitchen or living room: every
moment, every inch, every atom
of home felt as if sacred.

JUST SIT THERE

A frog on a lily pad am I—
inverted syntax and a love
of words my only uncommon
trait, so I do my best to avoid
spiritual pride, for who would
notice me anyway? Not a soul.
I just sit here on this lily pad
reciting the words of Shunryu
Sukuki: "A frog is very
interesting. He sits like us,
too, you know, but he does not
think that he is doing anything
so special." And I'm not.

When I bother to think, it's with
a small frog body that just happens
to house a brain and intentionality—
the only game in town: personal
awareness, biologically-based,
but no big deal, nothing to shake
a stick at, toss over your shoulder
for luck, or pretend to possess forever.

If something or someone annoys me
(and that does happen from time to time),
I do make a face, and if something
tempting comes along to eat, I will
snap it up, without moving a pace,
just remain here squatting on my
lily pad as still as I can be. If any thing
beautiful should happen by
(preferably a female frog) my thoughts
reach out to embrace her, but my toes

lie still, just dreaming of a life
we might share together if there
was room for more than one frog
on my lily pad.

Surrounded and embraced by all
that exists in this life, I feel I just
may be a small important frog part
of it—an instrument of peace,
although that role may smack
too close to spiritual pride for comfort,
so I try my best to disclaim it, and just
sit, a small frog on a lily pod—
nothing special.

POETRY

> "But granting that someone did say in all seriousness
> that the poets lie too much: he was right—we do lie too much ...
> We also know too little, and are bad learners: so we are obliged to lie."
> Nietzsche

Actuality excuses nothing—not even poetry.
The actual demands so much of our time,
and even curved space. Poetry may survive
as a strange sickbedfellow, but real, no longer
pretend, for real poetry is not just wishful
thinking, but a genuine marriage—in sickness
and in health—between you and the right words.

We may trace poetry's rich history back
to epic narrative (sung) made of hydrogen
and helium; some immense bathtub of visible
light (monuclier mating), high-mass stars
exploding, the birth of Earth, self-replicating
life, single-celled organisms, big brains
that sang songs about their history: what
and how and when and who they came to be.

            By 1300 B.C., in Egypt,
bored with Tall Tales and heroes, they turned
to overt lyricism, to love songs about another
discovery: the wonder of intimate love, romance,
and eventual death.

So here we are. Although I do write the stuff,
I seldom call myself "a poet," although
I do worship words, so I just may qualify
for canonization on that score, but only
as a technician ("Techne": the Greek word τέχνη,
a listener, engaged in "craftsmanship," or "art":
Michelangelo sculpted cannonballs, Charles
Peguy mended chairs.); just someone

(regardless of gender) who puts pants on one leg at a time—and writes a poem or two on occasion.

THE SOUNDS OF KAUAI

1.

Ireland boasts in song of forty shades
of green, but here in Kauai at least
four hundred hues of that color exist
on first sight, yet refuse to remain
content to be just something seen—for
they are converted on the spot
to a symphony, a suite, a full choir
of sublime sound.

          A host of birds
make their contribution to this
concert from every corner of the island—
first thing in the morning and all day long,
conducted by the wind, which is
the prime mover of all melody, not
just that of birds, but the constant dance
of ferns and fronds and small leaves that never
cease moving, sweetly swaying, until ...

the wind decides to *STOP*, to cease,
leaving all in abeyance, silence, a deep
lull of longing, yearning that asks
the fundamental existential question:
What next?

          A temperamental lover,
when the Kauai wind returns, it's riotous,
cacophonous, uncompromising.
What was an enjoyable caress of neck
or cheek or the loving stroke of a favored
limb becomes a savage slap in the face—
primitive, primeval (punishment
for the sake of having committed
some sin you can't recall?), a reminder

that life in the islands can be just
as fierce as it is friendly.

Kauai, on this, our return trip after
sixty years, is a quick-change artist,
still following its own will, not that
of those who've come to visit again.

2.

Sixty years ago, at age twenty-one
(and just recently married), my wife
Betty and I spent a honeymoon summer
living in a shack (of wood, not grass)
on the Wailua River on the island
of Kauai.

Caressed by soft winds then, our summer
home was located at the end of a narrow
dirt road that stemmed from
Kuamo'o Road, once known as
"The King's Highway," for the kings
of Kauai's *yesterday* had chosen
the Wailua River as *their* home,
making it "royal ground"—all
of Kauai's royalty having been
born there.

   The king, exalted, *pua ali'i*,
thought to be directly descended
from the gods, alone was allowed to walk
the spine of the ridge that became Kuamo'o Road.

    Betty and I
did not know any of this at the time,

and we possessed nothing resembling
or suggesting royalty ourselves, working
as short order cooks in a bowling alley
our host, our benefactor, started
on this island that was mostly plantation
country: pineapple and sugar cane
which narrow gauge trains still carried
to the mill.

        Often, we paddled
an orange canoe up the river to
the Fern Grotto, where I sang
"Ke Kali Nei Au" ("The Hawaiian
Wedding Song": "I will love you
longer than forever") to my young wife.

        No electricity
in the shack, just a crude gas stove,
and a shower beneath which we cavorted
passionately enough to conceive
a child (our first-born son) when we
got out. (For the kings of Kauai
waterfalls not fire stood for passion
and romance: "kahua i kawai":
"We two in the waters.")

        A narrow dirt road
beneath Kuamoʻo Road was all
that led to our own small home of love—
sheltered from any strong winds—and I
like to think the residents above us
on the King's Highway—those Hawaiian lords
of old (who were once obliged to kill
any stranger, unfortunate enough,
untimely enough to cross their shadow),
smiled upon us: two common naïve

twenty-one-year-old Mainland haole
city kids—those kings granting us,
it seemed, their ghostly good will.

3.

On our return trip, sixty years
later, the wild symphony of wind became
our constant companion, each day (and night),
replacing what we'd anticipated:
Betty's longed-for homage to Esther
Williams (in *Pagan Love Song*), her
backstroke Poipu swim postponed
(the beach was closed, the customarily
benign currents out of control,
a cloudless sky upstaged by
an obstinate gale)—but we didn't
complain, just grateful to be back
on the island where we "got our start,"
in spite of the weather.

                The intemperate
winds did provide continuous music
full of variety and surprise, and I
began to relish it, concocting
images for the range of effects:
palm fronds stroking the air that
surrounded them with increased passion,
like a couple steadily making love; or
(and this Betty found far-fetched): each tree
become a parody of human anatomy,
each tendon, ligament exposed—
the intricate network of interlaced sound
leaping from synapse to synapse, each
cell an echo of another.

Betty let me know
she found the image "In Kauai,
even sweat sings" unacceptable, but
after a restless wind-laced night,
she confessed she thought she'd heard
a concert of xylophones taking place
on the porch—which proved (in morning light)
to have been composed by a set
of wooden Hawaiian wind chimes, each
slender pipe so perfectly aligned
with the others (and of set pitch),
the whole provided a handsome folk song
melodic sequence filled with
nuance when the pipes met, and *kissed*.

4.

Paradise is never a given; it evolves,
it *becomes*, if it arrives at all.
Past and present, the always musical
winds of Kauai (as we learned
on our return) are as cruel as they
can be kind.

Ours is the same wind
that snapped the mainmast of Captain Cook's
ship, *The Resolution*, and sent him back
to Kauai for repairs, where he was not
as favorably received as before. At Kealakekua Bay,
now in *kapu* (taboo), hostile Hawaiians
greeted the "white god" and four marines
with spears, not leis, leaving them
dead after a brief skirmish.

These, *our* winds on our return,

are the same winds that perpetually
prevented King Kamehameha from
fulfilling his *hoʻohiki* (vow)
to "drink the water of Wailua, bathe
in the water of Namaimakua," and land
an army of 10,000 men and 1,500
canoes on Kauai to claim the island
for himself: braving the winds of Kaiei
Waho Channel which separate
Oahu from Kauai, but which forced him
to turn back with the pitiful remains
of his armada.

Our winds seem more sportive, playful,
contemporary 21st century Social
Media winds, over-produced, richly
choreographed for familiar effect,
worthy of Prime Time; but no, these
are, and are not, the same gusts
that carried ("the wind in his favor,
but waves breaking over the gunwales")
Liholiho, son of and successor to
Kamehameha, to Kauai, where
he met with Kaumualii, his father's
nemesis, who possessed "personal
beauty and gentlemanly manners,"
and could boast of the highest lineage
of any chief in all the islands—
who greeted Liholiho with kindness,
feasted and gifted him, and was then
kidnapped, this rightful King of Kauai,
invited on board the *Pride of Hawaii*,
Liholiho issuing secret commands
to raise anchor and up sails and head
for Oahu, Kaumualii now

"a prisoner of state," and forced
to marry the imperious Kaahumanu
(once the favored queen of Kamehameha),
who also made Kaumualii's son
her husband as well: father and son
"in her chains ... which were not
altogether silken."

The former King of Kauai, handsome,
tall, possessing a "noble Roman face,"
would breathe his last in May of 1824,
defunct at the age of forty-four, saying,
"I die with affection."

                    A blood bath
would follow on Kauai: ten days
of violence that left the island's men,
women, and children dead—all legitimate
chiefs deposed of their lands and deported,
scattered to ... the winds.

5.

This perfect place, gentle, isolated
island, Kauai, our sacred second home—
but just how *sacred* is it? The wild winds
suggest, "Don't ask; we shall make
believers of you on our own," and they
resume their sublime symphonic flux:
passages with the gentle, assuaging asylum
of slack key guitar, followed by a storm,
a dramatic outrage worthy of
Hector Berlioz at his savage best—strange
bedfellows perhaps, but not in the world
of music, where the most brazen
contrast sits side by side with the sexiest

juxtaposition: a quantum condition
in which point-like particles (or waves)
align themselves, strings or membranes
of sound, and bird calls mix with the subtle
speech of fronds—music rich with
the song of space and time.

The ancient kings of Kauai chose
the mouth of the Wailua River (where
Betty and I once lived) as their home—
one of the two most sacred spots
in all the Hawaiian islands: *Wailua
Nui Hoano* (The Great Sacred Wailua),
where two birthstones mark the spot,
stones shaped like the back of a woman
and her spread legs awaiting the birth
of kings, in a house of grass, such as
that Betty and I once lived in (but ours
of wood, not grass).

Was Kauai sacred? The island was ruled
by *moi*; kings or sovereigns who owned
all of the land in sight, who possessed
the power of life and death over all
their domain (lesser chiefs could only
commune with them at night), but kings
who could make an exception and cohabit
with commoners (such as Betty and me)
if they chose to—favored subjects who
did not prostate themselves at will,
or pay the price of death if they
crossed the sovereign's shadow.

And so we return, safely, to Kauai
after sixty years: to refresh
our sacred roots, and accept whatever
the weather allows (Betty not able

to swim until our very last day
on the island, but at Hanalei,
an ideal spot)—and we listen
with delight to the island's epic concert,
and travel up the Wailua River
just below the King's Highway, our shack
long gone, but Kauai's destiny
evident in every sound around us.

We count our many blessings, one
by one: two embodied spirits,
still in love, with a destiny that's all
our own, but shaped by the winds
of Kauai years (and centuries) ago.

At home in our own Garden of Eden,
our very own gracious Kingdom Come,
we lie in bed at night, and watch
and listen to the now mild winds
make dancing cubist shadows of
the Japanese Elm tree just outside
the window.

      A soft rain begins to fall,
with the free and easy drift of the soothing
music of slack key guitar—and soon we
are nested, and softly reside within
the bliss of windswept island sleep.

Source: *Kauai: The Separate Kingdom,*
Edward Joesting

William Minor was originally trained as a visual artist (Pratt Institute and U.C.-Berkeley), and exhibited woodcut prints and paintings at the San Francisco Museum of Art, the Pennsylvania Academy of the Fine Arts, the Honolulu Museum of Art, the Smithsonian Institution, and other museums and galleries. His woodcut prints incorporated the text of Russian, Modern Greek, and Japanese poetry—which he also translated.

Attracted by the "multimedia" work of William Blake, e.e. cummings, Kenneth Patchen and Shiko Munakata (and the voice of Dylan Thomas), he began to write poetry as a graduate student in Language Arts at San Francisco State (1963), producing his first book containing poems and woodcut prints, *Pacific Grove*, in 1974. Bill has, since that time, published six more books of poetry: *For Women Missing or Dead, Goat Pan, Natural Counterpoint* (with Paul Oehler—nominated for Pushcart Prize XI); *Poet Santa Cruz: Number 4; Some Grand Dust* (for which he was a finalist for the Benjamin Franklin Award), and *Gypsy Wisdom: New & Selected Poems*. His poetry has appeared in numerous journals and anthologies, as has his short fiction—which was selected for inclusion in *Best Little Magazine Fiction* (NYU Press) and *The Colorado Quarterly Centennial Edition*. A one-act play, *Contacts*, was performed at Monterey Peninsula College in California, and then published in *The Bellingham Review*.

A jazz writer with over 150 articles to his credit, Bill has also published three books on music: *Unzipped Souls: A Jazz Journey Through the Soviet Union* (Temple University Press), *Monterey Jazz Festival: Forty Legendary Years* (Angel City Press; Bill served as scriptwriter for the Warner Bros. film documentary based on the latter, same title as book), and *Jazz Journeys to Japan: The Heart Within* (University of Michigan Press). A professional musician since the age of sixteen, Bill set poems from *For Women Missing or Dead* to music and recorded a CD—*Bill Minor & Friends* (on which he plays piano, tenor guitar, and sings). A second CD, *Mortality Suite,* offers original poems and music. Bill was also commissioned by the Historic Sandusky Foundation to write a suite of original music and voice script based on a married couple's exchange of letters throughout the Civil War: *Love Letters of Lynchburg*.

A poem—"My Fingers Refuse to Sleep"—was published in *december* magazine, and, set to original music and sung by Jaqui Hope (with Heath Proskin on bass and Bill on piano), is available on YouTube: https://www.youtube.com/watch?v=RLqjmDeiz2s. The title poem from *Another Morning: Poems by William Minor* is available on YouTube (original music by Bill performed on piano, with Bill reciting the poem): "Another Morning by William Minor": https://www.youtube.com/watch?v=epJ7eFylCoQ.

In May, 2011, Bill was "first grand prize winner" in a national essay contest, "What Music Means to Me," sponsored by RPMDA (Retail Print Music Dealers Association). More biographical information and links are available at www.bminor.org.

www.ingramcontent.com/pod-product-compliance
Lightning Source LLC
LaVergne TN
LVHW041551070426
835507LV00011B/1047